# SONIA SOTOMAYOR

## A Little Golden Book® Biography

By Silvia López • Illustrated by Nomar Perez

The editors would like to thank Lisa Kathleen Graddy, curator, Division of Political History, at the National Museum of American History, for her assistance in the preparation of this book.

🌼 A GOLDEN BOOK • NEW YORK

Educators and librarians, for a variety of teaching tools, visit us at RHTeachersLibrarians.com
Library of Congress Control Number: 2021941289
ISBN 978-0-593-42743-9 (trade) — ISBN 978-0-593-42744-6 (ebook)
Printed in the United States of America
10 9 8 7 6 5 4 3 2 1

When Sonia Sotomayor was little, she didn't dream about being a judge. There were no judges or lawyers living in her public housing project in New York City. How could she dream of something she didn't know?

Sonia was born in New York City on June 25, 1954. Her parents, Celina and Juan, had come from Puerto Rico. They didn't speak English well and had very little money. But they were always surrounded by family.

Sonia loved her grandmother's weekly parties, especially Abuelita's delicious Puerto Rican food.

After eating, it was fun to play bingo and dance salsa with her cousins!

The only person who didn't go to many parties was Sonia's dad.

Papi loved his children. And baseball. He and Sonia were big Yankees fans. He was also a good cook. On Fridays, he took Sonia grocery shopping. But sometimes Papi drank too much. It affected his health and his behavior.

Mami worked long hours so that Sonia and her brother, Junior, could attend Catholic school. "You've got to get your education," Mami told them. "It's the only way to get ahead in the world."

One day, seven-year-old Sonia fainted at school. Doctors said she had diabetes. She needed injections of a medicine called insulin.

Sonia overheard her parents arguing about who would give her the injections. So Sonia climbed on a chair and got ready to clean the syringe by dropping it into boiling water.

"Sonia, what are you doing?" her mom cried.

"I'm going to inject myself, Mami," Sonia answered.

From then on, Sonia took charge of her diabetes.

Just before Sonia's ninth birthday, Papi passed away.

Mami stayed in her room after work, grieving in silence. Sonia spent many hours at the library. She liked reading about a girl detective named Nancy Drew. But she was lonely. One night, Sonia pounded on her mother's bedroom door and cried out, "Enough, Mami!"

The next day, Sonia and Junior came home to find Mami cooking. She wore a pretty dress and smelled of perfume. Sonia smiled. Things would get better.

With her savings, Mami bought a new set of encyclopedias. The books made Sonia's world "branch out in a thousand new directions." She focused on her schoolwork. She began to dream big dreams.

Sonia liked puzzles. She thought of being a detective or a lawyer, like on TV. Court cases were a lot like puzzles. She decided to study law. She promised herself that someday she would become a judge.

Sonia was one of the best students in her high school class. A friend encouraged her to apply to Ivy League colleges. She found out they were excellent schools, but expensive.

A government program called Affirmative Action helped good students from Black and Hispanic families who could not afford to pay for college. Not everyone agreed with the program. Some people asked why give those students an advantage? Sonia knew why!

While Mami studied to become a nurse, Sonia worked weekends and summers to help pay bills.

At the same time, she got great grades, took part in debate competitions, and won many awards.

All Sonia needed was a chance. The rest—success or failure—would be up to her.

In her first year at Princeton University, Sonia didn't do well on a written paper. One professor said she was mixing English and Spanish. Sonia decided to improve her English grammar. She organized her study time, and the hard work paid off. Sonia graduated college with the highest honors.

Sonia earned a law degree from Yale University in 1979. She worked as a lawyer for many years. Later, she became a judge, just like she had promised herself. In one case, she settled an argument between baseball players and team owners. She became known as the judge who saved baseball.

"You have to learn to **DREAM BIG DREAMS.** Education opened my eyes to what I could become."

In 2009, a new United States Supreme Court judge—called a justice—had to be chosen.

One night, Sonia's phone rang. It was
President Barack Obama! He told her he wanted
her for the job. Sonia caught her breath, then said
simply, "Thank you, Mr. President."

On August 8, 2009, as Mami and Junior watched, Sonia Sotomayor raised her hand and took an oath to "administer justice." She was now the third woman—and the first Latina—on the Supreme Court of the United States.

Sonia had dreamed big dreams—and made them come true.